THEY ATE

WHAT?!

The Weird History of Food

Richard Platt

MINNETONKA, MINNESOTA

Contents

First published in the USA in 2006 by
Two-Can Publishing
11571 K-Tel Drive
Minnetonka, MN 55343
www.two-canpublishing.com

Editorial Director: Jill Anderson
Cover Design: Brad Norr Design

Text copyright © Oxford University Press, 2006

This Americanization of *Would You Believe Marzipan Contains Cyanide? and Other Freaky Facts,* originally published in English in the UK in 2006, is published by arrangement with Oxford University Press.

Library of Congress Cataloging-in-Publication Data

Platt, Richard.
  They ate what?! : the weird history of food / Richard Platt.
    p. cm.
  Summary: "Describes humans' food choices, preparations, and mealtime etiquette over the course of history"—Provided by publisher.
  Includes bibliographical references and index.
  ISBN 1-58728-577-0 (hardcover : alk. paper) —
  ISBN 1-58728-578-9 (pbk. : alk. paper)
  1. Food—History—Juvenile literature. 2. Food habits—History—Juvenile literature. I. Title.
  TX355.P53 2006
  641.3'009--dc22
                              2006012843

1 2 3 4 5 10 09 08 07 06

Printed in China

WARNING: The recipes and practices in this book are for information only and should not be tried at home!

Introduction

WHAT'S YOUR FAVORITE food? And don't say hamburgers or pizza—they are so last year! Food can be much more interesting if you want it to be. How about tasty stir-fried locusts? Or roasted rat? Or even delicious dog stew?

People have made meals of these foods and many stranger ones. You may say "Yuck!" but why shouldn't we eat these things? After all, insects such as locusts are a lot like shrimp, except that they live on land. Rats live in holes and eat vegetables, just as tasty rabbits do. (OK, maybe you don't eat those either, but many people do!) Are you sure you could even tell the difference between dog stew and chicken stew?

Most people couldn't. In fact, ask anyone who has eaten something weird and wacky what it tasted like, and they will usually answer, "Just like chicken!" In the pages that follow, you can read and wonder about the weirdness of what we eat and how we eat it. If you are tempted to taste some of the things you read about, think of this book as a collection of menus, not recipes. Many of the dishes need special preparation. Some may make you ill, and others could even kill you. So if you don't know how to cook something properly, don't be tempted to try it.

Would You Believe...?

Why, how, who?
Why did zoo animals end up on the dinner table in Paris in 1871? How do tapeworms make people lose weight? Why do some people in Japan eat a fish that is deadly poisonous? Who were the first people to try hot chocolate? If you want to find out the answers, read on!

Ancient Menus

WHAT DID THE FIRST humans eat? We will never know for sure. Humans had lived for half a million years before anyone wrote a recipe book. But archaeologists have figured out roughly what was in these ancient people's meals.

They can tell what was on the menu thousands of years ago from gnawed bones and trash heaps. Occasionally, food scraps have survived in the stomachs of ancient bodies that have been preserved in mud or ice.

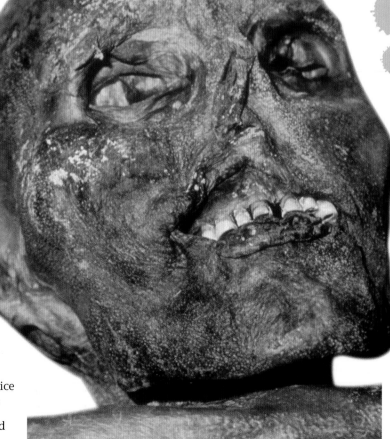

Frozen food ▲ ▶
The 4,000-year-old body of Ötzi the ice man was found in the Alps in 1991. Scientists discovered the remains of grains, red deer, ibex (wild goat), and vegetables inside his stomach.

Early humans did not have much choice when it came to food. They ate whatever they could hunt, pick, or dig up that would not poison them. As humans spread out across Africa and Asia, their **diet** changed. Meat was good when they could get it. Those near the coast ate fish and **shellfish.** And people everywhere ate plants.

◀ ▲ **Insect evidence**
Bits of beetles were found in ancient human feces in Nevada.

Wild and raw
The very earliest people ate mostly raw meat. One group, which lived in a cave near Peking, China, between 700,000 and 400,000 years ago, lived mainly on deer meat. Scientists also found in the cave a mix of human and wild beasts' bones. In this case, some think that "Peking Man" was the dinner, not the diner!

▲ **Wild food**
Peking Man may have eaten rhinoceros and tiger as well as wild pigs and sheep.

Passing through
One way to figure out what prehistoric people ate is by looking into their lavatories! Surprisingly, some of what we eat passes unchanged through our bodies. Bits of shell, fish scales, bones, hairs, charcoal, seeds, and pollen grains come out of our bodies pretty much in the same condition as they went in. The study of prehistoric poop even has a name: **paleoscatology.** Thanks to this science, we know, for example, that the ancient people who explored Lovelock Cave in Nevada snacked on insects when they got hungry.

▲ **Coprolites**
Paleoscatologists study ancient feces, which they call **coprolites.** Soaking coprolites in paint remover dissolves unwanted material, leaving just those vital clues to a prehistoric diet. It's hard to tell whether a coprolite comes from a human or another animal. The only sure way to find out is to look for fossilized parasites that live only in human hosts.

Roman
Banquet

Romans reclining ▶
Romans did not sit down to eat, as we do. Instead, they lay on couches grouped around the dining table. Slaves wiped their hands for them, poured wine, and brought food. They had other less pleasant tasks, too.

WHEN IT CAME TO FEASTING, nobody could beat the ancient Romans. The richest of them threw huge **banquets.** Guests gorged themselves for hours on rich dishes. Stuffed to bursting, diners wobbled from the room to be sick. Then they staggered back to eat some more.

Roman slave chefs competed to make their masters the best food in the city. Some of the dishes they cooked, such as roasted lamb, we still make today. But Romans also mixed foods in a way that we would find disgusting or just plain strange (see opposite).

Would You Believe...? Would You Believe...? Would You Believe...?

Clever cooks
Cleverness in cooking counted more than flavor in ancient Rome. Chefs made "a fish from a pig's belly, and a chicken from a knuckle of pork." They did this to show off, but also to hide cheap ingredients. Everything was seasoned with *garum*, a sauce made from fish rotted for a year.

Dormouse delicacy ▶
A favorite Roman dish was roasted dormouse dipped in honey and rolled in poppy seeds. The edible dormouse is slightly smaller than a squirrel. It was trapped in the wild and then fattened up in a pottery jar called a *glirarium*. The dormouse sometimes grew so fat on its diet of hazelnuts and acorns that the chef had to break the jar to remove it.

"When we lie down at a banquet, one slave wipes up the spittle; another, under the table, collects what the drunks leave behind"

● ● ● ● ● ● ● ● ● ● ● ● ● ● ● ●

ROMAN RECIPE

PORK COOKED "GARDENER STYLE"
(WITH FRESH VEGETABLES)

INGREDIENTS
One whole pig
Balls of minced chicken
Finely chopped roast thrushes (birds)
Little pork sausage cakes
Pitted dates
Glazed onions
Snails
Leeks
Beets
Celery
Cooked sprouts
Coriander
Whole peppercorns
Nuts
15 eggs

STEP 1
Remove the pig's bones through the mouth (to avoid breaking the skin) then stuff it with all the listed ingredients.

STEP 2
Thereupon sew it tight and roast in the oven.

Rich pickings

The cost of eating well ruined some wealthy Romans. One greedy man paid the equivalent of $9,800 for a single, perfect fish. Another, named Apicius, spent 60 million *sesterces* (6 tons of gold) on banquets. When he had only 10 million sesterces left, he killed himself, because he could no longer afford to live the life he enjoyed.

Fast food ▶
Only wealthy Romans ate huge meals. The poor ate mostly bread and a kind of porridge. They also bought take-out food from lunch counters like this one, preserved in the ancient town of Herculaneum, in Italy.

Medieval Mealtimes

MEDIEVAL DINERS certainly ate weird food. Birds were especially popular. Cooks roasted swans and baked blackbirds and seagulls in pies. Strange seafood was common, too. Porpoise, known as "sea pig," was a favorite, and so were whales and seals.

You might not have recognized these beasts on the table, though. Food was often mashed in the kitchen to make it easy to eat. Instead of plates, diners ate from stale slices of bread called "trenchers." Cooks added costly **spices** to dishes to show how wealthy the host was. Meat or fish dishes shared the table with sweet, sticky puddings. Pastry pockets nicknamed "coffins" contained all sorts of surprises!

▲ **Knight-shaped jug**
A jug of water was essential for rinsing greasy fingers!

The worst kitchen job was turning the meat. Sometimes a dog or goose ran in a wheel to spin the spit.

Special occasions
Most food was cooked simply in huge pots, but roasted meats and fish were served whole for special occasions. Important guests looked on as carvers cut the roasts—it was all part of the entertainment.

Food with feathers ▶
To make a showy dish for banquets, medieval chefs skinned peacocks, roasted them, then put them back in their colorful feathers for serving.

▲ Finger food
Everyone ate with their fingers, sometimes with the help of a knife or spoon. Table forks didn't exist. Cooks cut up most meat in the kitchen so that diners could easily eat it with their fingers.

◄ Cool cuisine
Servants rushed hot food from the kitchen to the table, but dishes were cold by the time they were served.

◄ Splatting and spoiling
Each different way of cutting meat and fish was given a special name. A carver would "unbrace" a duck, "splat" a pike, "display" a crane, "fin" a chub, "barb" a lobster, "spoil" a hen, and "dismember" a peacock.

9

Aztec
Appetite

I N 1519, SOLDIERS FROM Spain discovered ancient Mexico and its people, the Aztecs. They marveled at the strange produce on display in a vast outdoor market in the capital city. Stalls were piled high with odd foods, all with names that sounded like rattling cutlery to European ears.

Tecuitlatl (stone dung) was a cake made from pond slime. *Atepocatl* (tadpoles), newts, frogs, white worms, ants, slugs, and grasshoppers were also for sale. Most prized of all, there was *ahuauhtli* (water wheat). Spaniards brave enough to taste it said it was like crab **caviar,** but they felt sick when they discovered that the tiny eggs were laid by the bugs we call water boatmen.

Amazing city ▼
When Spanish soldiers first saw the Aztec's fabulous capital, Tenochtitlan, they gazed in wonder. It was built on an island in the middle of a huge lake. It was the cleanest and most beautiful city they had ever seen—far nicer than even the grandest towns in Spain.

The Aztec people prized chocolate so much, they even used it as money, counting out the cacao beans like coins

Xipe Totec ▶
To welcome spring rains for their crops, Aztec warriors dressed as their god Xipe Totec. They wore the skins of human victims, dyed yellow to look like corn.

Aztec food we eat now

Without the knowledge and skills of Aztec farmers, we would lack many of the foods that we enjoy today. Here are some of the plants and foods that Spanish expeditions brought back from Mexico and other places in Central America:

◀ Vanilla pods

▼ Avocados

▲ Tortillas

▲ Sweet potatoes

▲ Chocolate

◀ Beans

▲ **Vanilla**, a kind of orchid, was grown by the ancient Mexicans, who called it "black flower."
Mashed **avocado** was called *ahuacamolli.* Sound familiar?
Tortillas are corn flatbread; Aztec tortillas were bigger than those we eat today.
Sweet potatoes were brought back to Europe by the Spanish conqueror of ancient Mexico, Hernán Cortés.
Chocolate in ancient Mexico was made into a drink, flavored with hot spices and poured from a great height to froth it up like a milk shake.
Beans—both dried and green types—first grew in the area now known as Peru.

Hemmed in by the lake, Aztecs in Tenochtitlan had to make the most of every scrap of farmland and be inventive cooks. They dredged mud from the lake to make *chinampas* (floating gardens), and used the corn they grew in them to make tortillas and *atolli,* a kind of porridge. They also dined on rattlesnakes, weasels, mice, and armadillos. Fish, **game,** and turkey were treats.

Long Pig

Would You Believe…?

The raft of *Medusa*
When the French ship *Medusa* ran aground off the West African coast in 1816, 150 people escaped the wreck on a small raft. They had no food, and within days they began eating the bodies of those killed in fights. This cannibalism did not help them: just 15 were rescued.

PERHAPS THE WEIRDEST, most gruesome food that people have ever eaten is … other people. Or is it? After all, human flesh is only meat. Most of us would say "Yuck!" but in the distant past we would have been the hungry few. **Cannibals** (people who ate people) were common.

Archaeologists often find human bones cut by knives or cooked and cracked open, suggesting that someone ate the marrow inside. Even in recent history, there are tales of shipwreck and plane crash survivors eating the dead when hunger overcame disgust.

▲ **Patty Reed as an adult**

▼ **The Donner party**
The most famous American cannibals were in the Donner party. This group of settlers was trapped by snow in 1846. Some of them survived by eating those who had died. Patty Reed was eight years old when she was rescued from her icy ordeal.

◄ **Patty Reed's doll**

▲ **Scare tactics**
European explorers often told stories of cannibalism to the people they conquered to make it seem as if they were savages. Yet this picture of the Tupinamba people of Brazil shocked 16th-century Europeans—and helped justify cruel expeditions to "civilize" them.

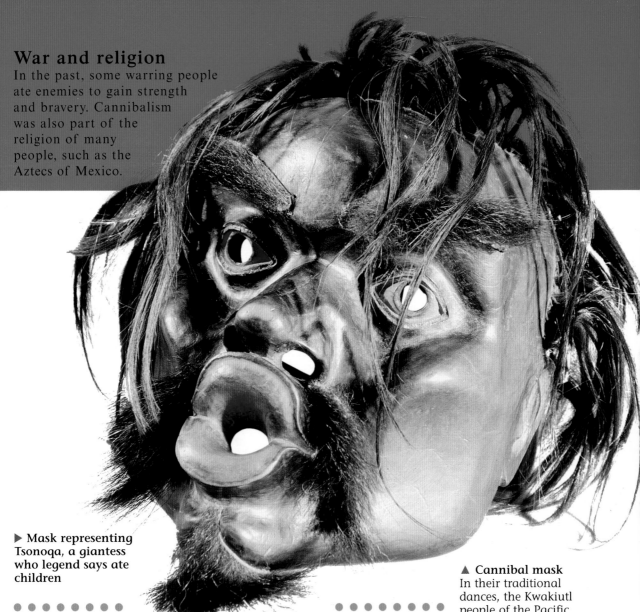

War and religion

In the past, some warring people ate enemies to gain strength and bravery. Cannibalism was also part of the religion of many people, such as the Aztecs of Mexico.

▶ Mask representing Tsonoqa, a giantess who legend says ate children

▲ Cannibal mask
In their traditional dances, the Kwakiutl people of the Pacific Northwest coast wore colorful and scary masks representing cannibal characters from their legends. One dancer, wearing the mask of the Hamatsa bird monster, actually bit and ate the flesh of those watching —or was it just a clever trick of the eye?

It is not easy to find out what people taste like, but there's a hint from New Guinea, where human meat was called "long pig." Recipes are even harder to find. The closest thing comes from Tlaxcala, in Mexico. When Spanish conquerors arrived in 1519, locals threatened to eat them. Eyewitness Bernal Diaz knew that they weren't joking: "They had already prepared the pots with salt and peppers and tomatoes."

Some scientists believe that almost all the world's ancient people ate human flesh

13

Feeding on Fido

Would You Believe...? Would You Believe...? Would You Believe...?

Friend or food
Don't fancy cat or dog? What about eating your guinea pig? Guinea pigs are a traditional treat in Peru, where they are fried or roasted and served as a dish called *cuy*. The meat tastes very much like rabbit and is better for you than chicken or pork. Peruvians eat 22 million guinea pigs each year.

" **I**'M SO HUNGRY I could eat a horse!" In a French restaurant, people might do just that. To many of us, eating a horse is a horrible idea, but if you were really hungry you would eat things you wouldn't touch when your stomach is full. When war cut off the food supplies in Paris in 1871, citizens ate their way through the city zoo.

▼ Bow-wow stew
Though selling and eating dog meat is against the law in Korea, *mung-mung tang* (bow-wow stew) is on many restaurant menus there. The government cracks down on lawbreakers when the nation expects many visitors from the West, such as in 2002, when Korea hosted soccer's World Cup.

▲ Horse on the menu
In the United States and in much of Europe, horse meat is sold only as dog food. In the past, though, many horses ended up on the table as food for humans, as this picture of a butcher's shop in Washington, D.C., shows. It was taken during World War II, in 1943.

The people of Paris ate all the animals in the zoo **except the lions and tigers (too fierce) and the monkeys (too human)**

Chef's cheval ▶
This hanging sign from a French butcher shop proudly announces "horses for sale." Horse butchers' shops in France, called *boucheries chevalines,* aren't as common as they once were.

The reason most of us don't eat horses, cats, and dogs is probably because we keep these animals as pets. We think of them as our friends—and almost human. Few people in Asian countries have pets, and cat and dog meat is popular there. People there tend to value animals for their skills (or as a food source), rather than as companions.

In 1996, starving people **in Argentina** caught and cooked stray cats **when their money ran out**

Pussy-tail stew
Some pets escape the pot because they are too useful to eat. In 1997, the government of Vietnam banned restaurants in Hanoi from serving "pussy-tail stew," because mouse and rat numbers in the city had soared.

15

What If It Wriggles?

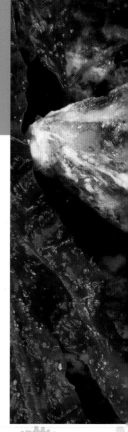

EVERYONE KNOWS FRESH FOOD IS good for you. So is the healthiest diet made up of food that is still alive? Diners in the world's best restaurants think so. The live oysters they eat squirm when soaked in lemon juice, and the lobsters are almost as unlucky. Restaurants keep them alive in aquariums, then cook them by plunging them—still alive—into boiling water.

◀ The human aquarium
Mac Norton, "the human aquarium," delighted European audiences in the early 19th century by swallowing live frogs and goldfish. He could also squirt water from his mouth into a bucket 20 feet (6 m) away.

CIRCUS BUSCH
Die Sensation:
Der unersättliche
MAC NORTON
Das menschliche
Aquarium

Oysters and lobsters are common dishes in the United States and Europe. But for a wider variety of live seafood, you need to travel to Asia.

In Japan, such dishes have a special name: *odori-gui* (dancing food). The name describes what it does on your plate—and in your mouth! The most popular "dancing" dishes are *kuruma-ebi* shrimps and *shirouo*, the tiny fish we call whitebait. They are served swimming in a bowl. You eat them with broth, vinegar, and soy sauce.

Eating an animal alive may seem cruel, but is it much less cruel to kill it first, then eat it?

Cruelty to animals?

A wriggling, dancing lunch may seem like a good argument for turning vegetarian. But those who eat live seafood say there is no cruelty in the meals. Experts claim that shellfish and fish don't have the brains to recognize pain. But not everyone agrees!

Army survival manuals recommend eating grubs live and wriggling

Wriggling whitebait ▲
A tourist brochure from Japan describes this dish of *shirouo* as being a seasonal **delicacy** "... delicious eaten raw as *odori-gui*. When we see the weirs (nets) for catching whitebait being set in the Nonai river, we know spring has finally come."

Food
Taboos

IT CAN BE HARD TO plan a dinner party if your friends have strict religious views. Hindus won't touch beef; Muslims and Jews don't eat pork. If the party is on a Friday, certain Christians will refuse to eat meat, so better serve fish— but not shellfish, because some Jews may not eat that, either.

Why do people choose their food according to how they worship? Some religious food **bans** can seem odd. They made more sense when they started long ago. Then many banned foods were scarce, so they were often too costly to eat.

▲ **Sacred cow**
Hindus in India will not eat beef, and they cherish their cattle. In Delhi, India's second largest city, 33,000 cattle roam free. They may seem useless, but most are important to the poor farmers who own them. They cost almost nothing to feed; oxen are cheaper and better for plowing than tractors; and cows provide vital milk.

Hungry Christians cheated the Friday meat ban with help from the barnacle goose

Fish or fowl? ▶
In the Middle Ages (5th–15th centuries), everyone thought that the barnacle goose hatched from a barnacle (a kind of shellfish), so it didn't count as meat. It was therefore on many a Friday menu in Christian households.

Beating the ban
Eating insects is outlawed
in the Old Testament of the
Bible, a text that is sacred
to both Jews and Christians.
However, there is an exception:
it's OK to eat locusts (see
page 32). This may be because
huge swarms of locusts ate
crops, causing **famine.** If
you can't beat them,
eat them!

Would You Believe...? Would You Believe...? Would You Believe...?

No place for pigs

Some religious food bans
may have started because
of the environment or
to protect people from
illness. It's no surprise
that Muslims and
Jews don't eat pork,
because keeping pigs
in the Middle East,
where both of these
religions began, used
up scarce resources
that humans needed.

Unclean pigs ▶
Under Jewish food rules, the pig is an unclean animal
and is not **kosher** (good to eat). This rule may have
started because pork sometimes contains tiny worms that
can make you ill if the meat is not cooked properly.

Preventing poisoning ▶
Shellfish is banned under Jewish food rules. This
may be because it contains poisons, and would also
have spoiled quickly in the heat of the Middle East.

Religious food bans have one great
advantage. By sticking to them, people
gain a sense of belonging. Missing out
on a food is something they share with
everyone of the same faith. It brings people
together and makes their faith stronger.

19

Awful Offal?!

Gummy candy ▶
If you ate a pig's trotter (foot), its sticky chewiness might remind you of gummy candy. That's because pig and cow feet are boiled up to extract gelatin—a vital ingredient in these squishy candies and other sweets.

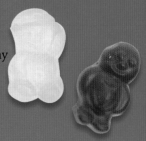

ARE ANY PARTS OF AN ANIMAL actually impossible to eat? Not many! Butchers used to boast that when they slaughtered a pig, all they wasted was the "oink." Today, things are different. Most meat counters sell only the lean, muscular parts of animals.

The rest of the animal, called **offal** or "variety meat," is hard to find. It turns up on the menu in some swanky restaurants—and in some of the cheapest. If the thought of chewing on an animal's liver, tongue, ear, or tail makes you gag, read no further. But offal can be delicious. Indeed, you may eat it more often than you realize.

Hidden offal

Offal is usually hard to find in supermarkets, but it is not thrown away. It is used up in all kinds of **processed** meat products, especially in cheap processed meats. To find out more, turn to pages 40–41.

▲ Ox or beef?
At the butchers, a bull gets two names. The better cuts are beef, but the offal is ox, such as oxtail. The meat has two different names because people in England once spoke two languages. The wealthy spoke French and called what they ate *boeuf*. The poor ate the leftovers and used the English word, ox.

Would You Believe...?

Too much of a good thing
Offal, and particularly liver, is high in vitamins and minerals, but you can have too much of a good thing. Farm animals' liver is fine, but steer clear of polar bear liver. It contains poisonous levels of vitamin A: 50 times as much as beef liver. Eating it has killed Arctic explorers.

You can play with offal
as well as eating it:
inflated pigs' bladders
make great balloons

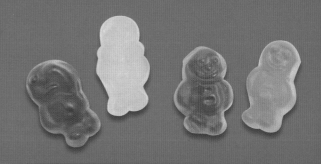

▼ Trotter casserole

Pigs' trotters are a delicacy if they are well prepared. If the idea makes you feel queasy, remember that a foot is just a joint down from a knee, which you may have enjoyed as pork knuckle.

◀ The haggis

Scotland's **haggis** is an offal delight: a sheep's lungs, heart, and liver stuffed inside its stomach for cooking. Homemade haggis is best, but it's not easy to find the ingredients. Lungs are banned in the United States, and few butchers sell stomachs.

LET'S TAKE A TOUR of the many parts of a pig that you can eat (but probably haven't).

At the very front, the pig's **snout** is a delicacy that is especially prized in Spain; in Poland, it's served up with soup.

The **ears** are a chewy delight: coated with breadcrumbs, they are deliciously crisp.

Lower down on the face, the **cheeks** are like fatty bacon. They are served as "Bath chaps" in Britain.

The **tongue** is rich meat that is delicious pressed like a ham and sliced.

Pork **brains** in milk gravy are traditionally served on scrambled eggs in the southern U.S.

Moving on down, pig **intestines** are usually filled with seasoned meat to make sausages. Today, only the best sausages are made from pig guts.

The **heart, kidneys,** and **liver** can all be eaten, but some people find the flavor a little strong.

At the very end of the pig, the **tail** can be a tasty treat. You might see pigs' tails dyed pink and piled high on Afro-Caribbean market stalls.

Vampire
Fare

IN SCARY VAMPIRE stories, thirsty demons bite helpless victims and drink their blood. Vampires—who legend says must drink human blood or die—exist only in storybooks. But the stories at least get one detail right: blood is a nourishing food.

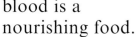

◀ **Black pudding**
Blood by the pint may not sound tasty, but food made from blood can be. In the hungry past, butchers collected the blood of slaughtered animals. They mixed it with cream or oats and fat and packed it into intestines to make a black sausage. The town of Mortagne-au-Perche in Normandy, France, holds a *foire au boudin* (black pudding fair) every March. There is also an annual black-pudding throwing event in Manchester, England. You can't buy it in the United States, though.

When Italian traveler Marco Polo (1254–1324) visited China 700 years ago, he marveled at the country's Mongol warriors. "They will ride for ten days without taking a meal," he wrote. "They drink the blood of their horses. They open a vein and let the blood jet into their mouths."

◀ **Vlad the Impaler**
The vampire in Bram Stoker's famous story *Dracula* is based on a European prince, Vlad Dracula (1431–1476). He was nicknamed "Vlad the Impaler" for his habit of impaling (spiking) his enemies on poles. Those who escaped from Vlad spread terrible stories about him, leading to legends of blood-drinking. But Dracula is a hero in his native Romania and is remembered as cruel but fair.

Masai meals

Cattle are both food and money to the wandering Masai people of East Africa. When milk runs short, they mix it with blood drawn from their cows' veins.

A diet of blood ▲ ▶
Masai people eat almost nothing but beef, cow's blood, and milk. They draw blood by firing an arrow at a cow's neck. They collect the blood in a gourd (a hard-skinned fruit) or a cup. The wound is plugged, and the cow's health is not affected. Neither is the health of the Masai. Though their diet is high in the fats that usually cause heart disease, the herbs they use in cooking keep them fit.

Most of us would draw the line at blood fresh from the vein, but as a soup, blood can be delicious. In Sweden, goose blood is the main ingredient for *Svartsoppa* (black soup), a traditional dish that's popular on St. Martin's Eve (November 10). It tastes a bit like rich gravy, and it's not difficult to prepare—as long as you remember to add vinegar to the blood to keep it from clotting!

If blood turns you off, don't watch when your mom cooks a roast: that great gravy flavor comes from "pan juices"— blood, in other words

23

You
Dirty Rat!

F AR FROM BEING dirty, rats are "well tasted and wholesome meat, seeing that their food is entirely vegetable, and that they are clean, sleek, and plump."

The Victorian author who wrote these words was trying to persuade his readers to eat a wider range of animals. With rodents, he bit off more than he could chew, because since Roman times, Europeans (and, later, Americans) have never been enthusiastic about eating rats and mice. In other parts of the world, people are not so choosy.

Barbecued rat ▲
Some small rodents can be eaten whole, barbecued and served with a dip. Grilled rat with baby onions was once a traditional dish in western France.

◄ Giant rat
The ultimate edible rat is the South American capybara, the world's largest rodent. It is 4 feet long (1.25 m) and can weigh as much as an adult woman. The capybara is raised for food on ranches in Venezuela. Its meat is very low in fat and is usually eaten either dried or salted.

Meaty treats
In a field in India, some Irula people prepare to catch their dinner. They light straw in clay pots to make smoke. They blow this down holes in the ground to drive out field rats. Some of the rats end up in their cooking pots, along with rice the rats have hoarded underground.

If the Inuit catch several mice, they run a piece of twig through them and without stopping to skin them, they broil them over the fire

The flying mouse ▶

Bats are like mice with wings, and are just as edible—they are popular barbecued in Burma and Thailand. Fruit bats are a pest in parts of northern Australia, where aboriginal people eat them grilled over hot coals. Don't be tempted to catch and eat bats yourself, though. They are rare and protected in many places, and some can carry disease.

In ancient China, rats were called "household deer" and were a treat. Inuit people were fond of roasted mice. Today, rodents make a welcome addition to the diet of many people who might otherwise never taste meat.

▼ Sleek and tasty

Field rats are not the scrawny beasts of city sewers. They are sleek, healthy, vegetarian—and tasty. Eating one is no odder than eating rabbits or hares, which also burrow in fields and destroy crops.

Extinction
on a Plate

OUR GREED FOR FISH FILLETS may soon wipe out the ocean's fish, and some land animals face the same end. Unless we choose our food more carefully, we'll eat some of the world's most wonderful creatures into extinction, and they'll be gone forever.

Many fish are being battered to death in the deep-fat fryer. Cod, for example, were once so common that fishermen on Newfoundland's Grand Banks just lowered baskets into the water to catch the fish. Some were bigger than the men who caught them. Today, there are almost no cod left there.

▲ **Kinder caviar**
Caviar is the egg of the sturgeon fish, which is being wiped out by over-fishing. Each tiny egg you eat means one sturgeon fewer in the sea. An alternative to caviar is avruga—specially treated eggs of the common herring.

◀ **Whale burger**
Scientists in Japan say they kill whales only to study them, but the meat of the whales is then sold as food. The Japanese government's plans to kill more minke whales may destroy these graceful giants of the ocean.

Would You Believe...?

A heavy price
Just one bite of beluga **caviar** (the eggs of beluga sturgeon) can cost more than $35! The true price of this delicacy is higher still, because the number of sturgeon is shrinking. The Convention on International Trade in Endangered Species (CITES) has agreed to strict limits on the catching of these fish.

Endangered on land

Hunting for food does not always put land animals and birds in danger of extinction. But hunting isn't the only risk facing the world's rare wildlife. Other human activities, such as cutting down forest trees, also threaten rare creatures. Hunting just finishes the job.

▲ Dead as a dodo
Huge, clumsy, and unable to fly, dodos once thrived on Mauritius—until Dutch sailors discovered this Indian Ocean island in about 1600. The birds had no fear of people, so they were easy to catch and cook. Within 75 years, the dodo was extinct.

◄ Bushmeat
Chimpanzees in West Africa may be extinct within 40 to 50 years. The illegal hunting and eating of apes, known as the **bushmeat** crisis, is having a great effect on the rate of decline of this creature. Deforestation, human settlement, and disease add to the problem.

◄ Mammoth menu
Overhunting helped to kill off many giant beasts of the Stone Age. If our ancestors had known a bit more about conservation, we might still be eating mammoth steaks to this day.

Farming won't save **wild fish from extinction: to produce 2 pounds of farmed fish, it takes 8 pounds of** fishmeal—food made from wild fish

Mud Pudding

Orinoco explorer ▶
German explorer Alexander von Humboldt was astonished in 1800 when he saw Ottomac people on the Orinoco river in South America eating mud. "They swallow every day very considerable quantities to appease their hunger."

EVERY KID ENJOYS MAKING mud pies. And a few of us never grow out of the habit. Some people eat mud just because they like the taste of it. Others say it makes them feel good. In some areas, women who are pregnant like to eat mud.

Mud fans are choosy about where it comes from. They dig mud from deep below the ground, where the soil is safer to eat. In Africa, earth from termite hills is a popular choice; it's sold in city markets.

Eating a little mud may help children to develop the ability to fight off disease

Keeping hunger away

In times of famine, more people get a taste for mud. When German and Austrian miners of the early 20th century could not afford butter or flour, they replaced them with earth and clay.

◀ Why do young kids eat dirt?
It's no use asking them. They will just stare at you as if the answer is obvious. Scientists have estimated that even children who eat dirt accidentally—from sucking dirty fingers or eating food that has fallen on the ground—swallow up to a teaspoonful a week.

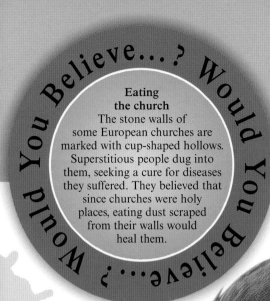

Eating the church
The stone walls of some European churches are marked with cup-shaped hollows. Superstitious people dug into them, seeking a cure for diseases they suffered. They believed that since churches were holy places, eating dust scraped from their walls would heal them.

▼ **Acorns and mud gravy**
Native American people from California used to collect acorns that contained poisons called tannic acids. Grinding the acorns and mixing them with clay removed three-quarters of the poisons, making them safe to eat.

Birds and beasts do it, too ▶
Animals such as this South American macaw have an instinct for eating soils that are rich in useful minerals. Places where these soils occur are famous for the animals they attract. The town of French Lick, in southern Indiana, is named for a mineral "lick" that attracted animals.

Useful minerals

Some muds contain minerals such as magnesium, iron, and zinc. These are missing from the diet of some people. Mud can also help remove natural poisons from plants, making them safe to eat.

Eating mud might seem crazy, but there are good reasons to do it. Clay settles and calms upset stomachs. You may have even eaten some yourself—a popular remedy sold by pharmacies contains kaolin, or white clay. But just because some mud is sometimes good for some people, not all mud is good for everyone. Soil often contains poisons and other unhealthy things, so don't just dig in and eat.

29

Snappy Snacks

Cancer cure ▶
In Guatemala, there once was a belief that eating a live lizard cured cancer. Scientists visited the town of Amatitlan in 1780 to look into the claim, but there is no record of their research.

SLITHERING, SCALY, SLIMY, or just plain dangerous, amphibians and reptiles are not popular choices for dinner. But frogs, lizards, turtles, snakes, and crocodiles are no strangers to the cooking pot. They were once an important part of the diet everywhere in the world. In Asia and South America, people still eat them with gusto.

Turtles used to be a common delicacy on European tables. Salty sailors in the Caribbean feasted on them. So what put us off? Perhaps it's what they look like. Some reptiles have fearsome faces. And compared to fur and feathers, scaly, horny, or slippery skin seems unnatural. It doesn't make the meat less tasty, though.

Fewer frogs
Killing frogs for food has made them scarce. It also has let insects that frogs eat multiply in number, threatening crops. So don't *jump* at the chance if you see frogs' legs on the menu!

A taste for frogs' legs earned the French a rude national nickname

◀ **Iguanas**
Never as popular as turtles because of their looks, iguanas are actually quite tasty. They have tender white flesh, and their fat is a delicacy. However, according to one diner, "When one of its paws happens to stick up in the dish, it reminds one too much of the alligator to eat it with any great relish."

◄ Gators on a plate
Each year, American farmers raise 220,000 alligators on ranches in Florida and Louisiana. Alligators raised as food are not endangered, and their meat is low in **cholesterol**, so it's healthy to eat.

Rattlesnake and alligator steaks are on a few menus in the American West. But most of us would still snap "No!" if offered a crocodile sandwich. It's probably a good thing, too. Our ancestors' taste for roasted tortoise and turtle almost wiped out some species.

Would You Believe...? Would You Believe...? Would You Believe...?

Turtles
Tortoises and turtles became popular dishes among wealthy Londoners in the 18th century. When a pub cooked up a giant turtle in 1753, a wall of the brick oven had to be removed to fit it inside. By the 19th century, Britain imported 15,000 a year, some weighing more than 330 pounds (150 kg).

Snake steaks ▼
A snake is a good food source, especially in deserts, where other game is scarce. Kalahari bushmen are preparing this snake for the table, but you can also find snake in restaurants from Kansas to Texas, where "Rattler Roundups" are a tourist attraction.

▼ Crunchy critters
Deep-fried grasshoppers
make a tasty, crunchy
snack! Mmmmmm.

A Diet
of Insects

HOW MANY INSECTS did you eat today? More than you imagine! There are fly eggs in fruit juice, maggots in pizza sauce, and insect parts in peanut butter. Food safety laws recognize that it isn't possible to remove all insects from food. They allow six insect parts per 20 grams (0.7 oz) of peanut butter.

There is nothing wrong with eating insects. In fact they make very good food. In parts of southern Africa, insects supply people with two-thirds of the **protein** they need, and in Southeast Asia, insects are a favorite street snack.

Anyone for locusts?

These large grasshoppers eat whole fields of crops—but we can fight back by eating them! Just remove the wings and back legs and boil until soft (about half an hour). Then stir-fry in sesame oil with garlic and hot peppers. Sprinkle with soy sauce and serve with salad and crusty bread.

▲ **Yes, please!**
This girl is trying a fried cricket as part of a program called "Global Kitchen."

People eat insect dishes because they are traditional **and** delicious

Leggy lunch ▶
Strictly speaking, spiders are not insects, but they can make excellent snacks. Spiders were first eaten in Cambodia when people ran short of other foods, but they are now considered to be a delicacy.

Other creepy crawlies

Crickets, grasshoppers, and locusts all belong to the same animal family, but they are not the only creepy crawlies that can be used to make a meal. Spiders, dragonflies, and worms can be found on the menu, too.

▲ Flying food

On the island of Bali in Southeast Asia, hunting dragonflies is an enjoyable sport—with a tasty bonus. The insects are very hard to catch, so hunters coat the tips of "whippy sticks" with sticky tree sap to trap the dragonflies. Then they wrap the dragonflies up in a banana leaf and grill them.

TODAY'S MENU

Starters

Insects and other creepy crawlies are ideal for snacks and appetizers. You don't need a knife and fork. Just pick them up in your fingers! Most insects have a tasty texture contrast. The outer shell is deliciously crunchy. The inside is moist, soft and often creamy or sweet.

Scorpion snack
Cooking takes the sting out of its tail!

Thai sour ant eggs
Biting bursts the thin skin, releasing a soft, cheesy center.

Main courses

Insects make a perfect ingredient for a satisfying, healthy meal. Maggots, for example, contain three times as much protein as the best beef. Insects are also ideal diet foods. Grasshoppers in particular are very low in fat.

Diving beetle
Deep fry, but remember to pull off the wings before eating.

Moth cakes
Singe off legs and wings, grind to a fine powder, mix with water to a make a paste, and bake.

Desserts

Why stop at **savory** foods? There's no reason why you can't eat insects for dessert as well! Some, such as the honey ant, would never have gotten their name if people did not know they were tasty and sweet to eat. Other insect desserts need help from sugar and chocolate.

Cricket lollipop
Clear melted sugar on a stick shows off the treat trapped inside.

Chocolatey grubs
Lightly cook grubs, dry carefully, and dip in chocolate for a sweet treat.

I Think I'll Go Eat Worms

N EED TO LOSE WEIGHT? WHAT about a meal that is no more fattening than the best beef, but has three times the **nutrients**? This amazing diet food is the humble maggot. Maggots are insects in disguise. They will turn into flies when they are older. Maggots (and all insects) are members of a group of animals called invertebrates—creatures without backbones.

Slipping down ▶
Most people find that land slugs are too disgusting to eat. Sea slugs, on the other hand, seem to slip down quite easily. Known as sea cucumbers, they are so popular in Chinese restaurants that some species are now endangered.

Worms, snails, and slugs are invertebrates too, and all of them are edible. But only the snail has made it onto classy restaurant menus. Worms and slugs haven't been as popular.

The popularity of snails as food led to "snail rustling" in Britain in 2005

Would You Believe...?
Snails
As *escargots*, snails are a popular dish in France. Feeding them on lettuce leaves for four days cleans dirt from their guts, and soaking them in salt and vinegar gets rid of the slime. Then it's just a matter of boiling and baking with garlic butter. But don't eat snails from the garden. They may contain poisons.

◄ **Silkworm kebab**

The fine threads that are woven into silk cloth come from silkworms. They are not really worms—they're grubs, or juveniles, of a large type of moth. The grubs spin the thread into cocoons when they are ready to change into moths. Factory workers who unwind the thread get a tasty bonus, for the grubs are delicious. Because so many countries produce silk, there are lots of recipes. Grubs are good boiled, fried, roasted, baked, steamed, or grilled on skewers, as shown here.

Mopane worms ▶

Many people in Botswana, Zimbabwe, and parts of South Africa enjoy the grubs of the emperor moth. Called mopane worms, the caterpillars are tasty when boiled or fried. But first, the cook squeezes out the guts.

Grub's up

Most insects pass through a larval stage between egg and flying critter forms. For hungry people, the larvae, also called grubs or maggots, have several advantages. They are easy to catch, many have a high food value, and they don't have lots of bits to get stuck between your teeth.

To get used to the idea of putting a maggot in your mouth, talk to anglers. Some of them use maggots on their hooks, and in winter, they may warm them in their mouths to make them wriggle. It's a step away from chewing and swallowing. Good cooking turns them from a snack into a meal.

Witchetty grubs ▶

Native Australian people find witchetty grubs in the roots of the acacia, also called the witchetty bush. Ten large grubs provide an adult with enough protein for a day. They are eaten raw or roasted over a very low fire.

35

Dining
with Death

OUTSIDE A HUNDRED restaurants in the Japanese city of Tokyo hang strange lanterns. They are made from the inflated skins of blowfish. These signs show that the restaurants serve blowfish, or **fugu,** a luxury **sushi** (raw fish) dish. It is not the flavor of fugu that makes it special—it doesn't have much taste. The attraction is that the blowfish contains a deadly poison.

▲ Dangerous nuts
Cycad nuts are a traditional food source for Australian Aborigines. The nuts look delicious, but they are poisonous unless they are prepared properly. To make them edible, cooks crack open the shells, pound the nuts inside to a paste, soak or wash the paste in water, then make it into bread.

There's enough poison in one fugu fish to kill 30 people—and 20 Japanese people die each year from eating it

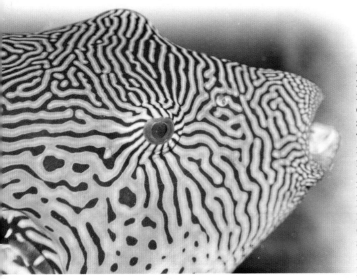

◄ Blowfish blowout
Fugu is one of the most expensive fish in Japan, so people order it as a way of showing off their wealth. The danger involved in eating fugu also makes it popular. Most people killed by fugu prepared the fish at home: they did not have the skill needed to remove all the poisonous parts.

Eating fugu is more of a dare than a dinner. Only careful preparation from a trained chef saves diners from a swift death. But people eat other poisonous foods for more sensible reasons, such as nourishment. For example, manioc is the main food of 600 million people around the world, but it contains a strong poison called cyanide.

◄ Don't eat your greens
Some "greens" should not be eaten! Rhubarb leaves contain oxalic acid, which can damage your kidneys if you eat it. And all parts of the potato plant except the potato itself contain poison. Avoid the potatoes, too, if the white areas turn green.

Also called cassava, manioc is made from a starchy plant root. But you can't just cook and eat the root. Just a slice or two would kill you. It has to be grated and strained first, to squeeze out the poison. Then it can be processed into tapioca, a familiar pudding. Countless other foods like manioc contain poison in small amounts. Some of them are very popular.

Would You Believe...? Would You Believe...? Would You Believe...?

Deadly decoration
Marzipan, used in desserts and cake decorations, contains the poison cyanide. This comes from the bitter almonds that flavor the paste. Marzipan is one of the few foods for which there are permitted levels of cyanide, but you would have to eat an awful lot of it to get sick.

Stone fruit ▲
The pits of apricots, plums, and cherries, and the seeds of apples contain cyanide. Just 15 apricot kernels (the soft center, inside the pit) are enough to kill a child. Fortunately, the kernel is hard to remove.

Incredible
Inedibles

DON'T TRY THIS AT HOME! Risking **indigestion** and injury, people eat the most unlikely things. Sword-swallowers and fire-eaters sound the worst, but they don't actually eat anything. The long blades come straight back out, and the flames never go down in the first place. Others make a meal of money, pebbles, cutlery, and almost anything else they can fit in their mouths.

Some people have forced down objects to hide them—swallowing coins rather than give them up to robbers. Others have a mental illness called pica and can't resist eating strange things. But most people who swap meat and greens for metal and glass do so for money.

A sharp appetite ▲
Expert sword-swallowers can swallow a blade 2 feet (62 cm) long. Sliding it down brings the mouth, throat, and stomach into a straight line. They train themselves not to choke, and the blunt sword does the rest.

Eating everything
Doctors call the ability to eat non-food items "polyphagia." Medical studies have shown that although smaller objects soon pass through, bigger ones stay in the body and cause injuries.

It can be dangerous just to watch someone eat fire

◀ **Fire-eaters**
Touching torches to their tongues, fire-eaters risk burns, but they don't actually eat fire. A coating of saliva protects their mouths against the flames. People have to go to fire-eating classes to learn how to perform this dangerous trick.

Hearty eater ▲
Frenchman Michel Lotito eats TV sets, grocery carts, and bicycles. He took two years to eat a light aircraft. "Monsieur Mangetout" (Mr. Eat-all) can eat so much metal because his stomach lining is twice the normal thickness.

38

As early as the 18th century, entertainers ate stones to draw crowds. One advertised that "...after the stones are swallowed they may be heard to clink in the belly the same as in a pocket!" Not to be outdone, his hungry rivals ate knives, forks, spoons, and broken glass.

▼ **Gut reaction**
If you are still hungry at the end of a meal, don't eat the cutlery. X-ray photographs of people who eat metal objects show where they end up. X-rays have also proven that sword-swallowers are not magicians: they really do put the blades down their throats.

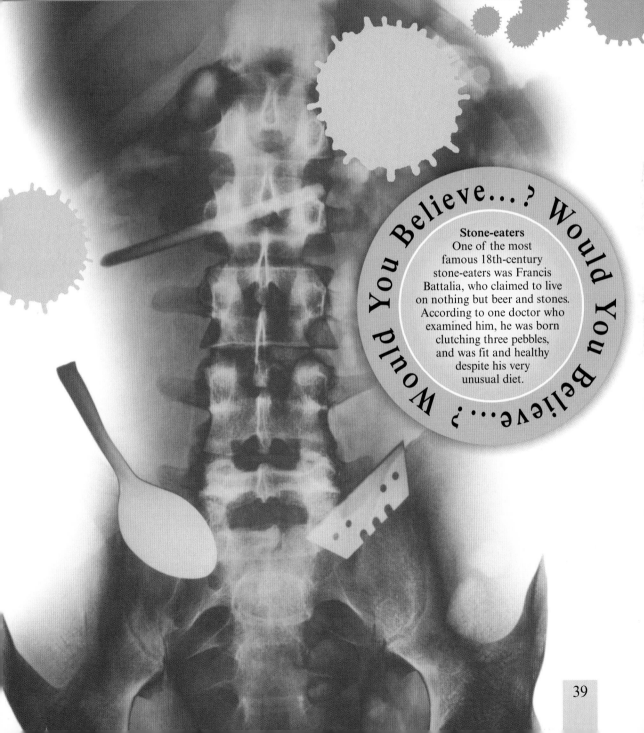

Would You Believe...?

Stone-eaters
One of the most famous 18th-century stone-eaters was Francis Battalia, who claimed to live on nothing but beer and stones. According to one doctor who examined him, he was born clutching three pebbles, and was fit and healthy despite his very unusual diet.

Farms
or Factories?

THE FOOD WE EAT EVERY DAY tastes great, but what's actually in it? You can find some answers by reading package labels, but they don't tell you everything. For instance, cheap chicken nuggets, burgers, and hotdogs often contain something called **mechanically separated meat.** It's a watery paste made by scraping or washing leftover meat from bones.

Meat is not the only food product that hides unpleasant secrets. Other processed foods are flavored with chemicals. That delicious pie you ate last week, for example, tasted really strongly of apple. However, its flavor may have come from a chemical called Ethyl-2-methyl butyrate.

Chemical traces ▲
Even real fruit can contain traces of the chemicals sprayed on it to keep bugs off. That's why it's best to wash fruit before you eat it.

Factory farming
As supermarkets pay less and less for the food they sell us, some farmers take dangerous shortcuts to keep profits up. In crowded fields and sheds, diseases spread rapidly between stressed animals.

◄ **Chicken run**
Even in the cleanest chicken processing factories, the contents of birds' intestines sometimes spill onto the meat. This spreads a germ called campylobacter to about half of all chickens. Careful cooking kills the germs, making the meat safe. But if the meat is not cooked properly, anyone eating it gets an upset stomach—if they are lucky. The unlucky ones die.

40

Ground meat often contains bones, skin, gristle, offal, and all sorts of artificial flavors

Fast food ▲
Even "pure beef" hamburgers may have been made from the meat of cattle that were fed blood, or newspaper and sawdust from poultry-barn floors. Beef cattle are naturally vegetarians and should eat only grass and grain.

There are good reasons why the food we eat is not all it seems to be. If farmers did not spray crops, food would cost more, and fruit and vegetables would look less perfect. And if food processors did not add chemicals, food would not keep so well. If we want purer food, we will all need to pay a little more, shop more often, and put up with odd-shaped carrots.

Fads and Fasts

Dieting and detoxifying ▶
There have been so many crazy diets, it's hard to sort out truth from fiction. Eating just orange-colored foods, having a spoonful of ice cream every two hours, and drinking lots of ice water have all been suggested as ways to lose weight or clear the body of **toxins**. What's next—a diet of foods that start with *C*?

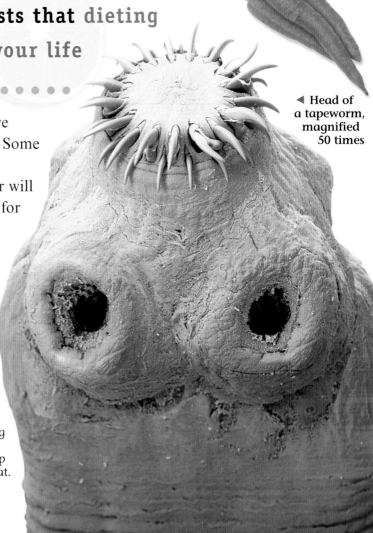

◀ Head of a tapeworm, magnified 50 times

DIETING REALLY BEGAN ABOUT 150 years ago, when London coffin-maker William Banting grew so fat that he had to walk downstairs backward. On his doctor's advice, he cut out sugar and starch and lost 50 pounds (23 kg). He then wrote the world's first diet book.

If you are only a little overweight, some research suggests that dieting can shorten your life

Since Banting's time, people have come up with ever-crazier diets. Some even try to starve their way to a slimmer figure. But as any dieter will tell you, nothing seems to work for long. Scientists now know that eating less can actually make people fatter. Their bodies get used to less food, so when the diet ends, they pile on the pounds again.

Eating worms
In the 1950s, opera star Maria Callas lost 62 pounds (28 kg) in one year, allegedly after swallowing a tapeworm, which grew in her gut. Diet pills holding tapeworm eggs were on sale in the U.S. at the time, but she may have picked up the parasite by eating undercooked meat.

A Light Repast

Fasting

Starvation diets are a fashionable way to get thin and **detoxify** the body. But going without food robs the body of energy, making it hard for organs to work properly. Waste stays inside the body longer, and you get headaches and bad breath. **Fasting** for more than a day is dangerous for young people and those with **diabetes** or heart disease.

▲ **Diet food and drinks**
For decades, makers of weight-reducing foods have promised to make dieting quick and easy. But products such as Allen and Hanbury's 1905 Diet Health Drink ("Just mix with hot water!") were expensive to buy and boring to eat. Few people who ate them would have gotten any thinner.

At least one-quarter of us diet, and there are nearly 13,000 diet books to tell us how to do it. Many of them outline fad diets that won't help readers. Some of these diets are actually dangerous. We believe them because we want an easy way to get thin. Sadly, there is no easy way, but there is a simple way. Anyone can lose weight by exercising more and eating less. The catch is that you must do this all your life, not just for a few weeks or months.

In the 17th century, only the wealthy could afford to eat well, so it was not fashionable to be skinny. Women in paintings of that time look plump to us!

What's So Weird about That?

PERHAPS YOU HAVE SMILED or gasped, or felt slightly sick as you read this book. These are perfectly natural reactions, but don't be too quick to laugh at other people's meals. Often, their strange dishes are as nourishing as anything you eat. And they might find your diet as disgusting as you find theirs.

In many parts of Asia, for example, nobody drinks or cooks with milk. Vietnamese people find cheese, butter, milk, and cream as horrible as we might find stir-fried grasshoppers.

Would You Believe...? Would You Believe...?

Scary supper
Strange new foods take a while to get used to. When a new food plant was brought to Europe in the 16th century, few people liked it. Two hundred years passed before many farmers grew it. Even in 1770, people in Germany preferred to starve rather than eat it. What was it? The potato!

◀ Roasted ram
In parts of Mongolia, roasted sheep's head is served up on special occasions. The cheeks and eyeballs are delicacies. They are usually offered to the guest of honor.

Yucky or yummy?
Even if nothing you have read makes you hungry, maybe you will think twice before turning up your nose at a strange dish. Whether we say "Yuck" or "Yum" depends on what we are used to eating. Remember, if something swims, flies, crawls, or walks, somebody somewhere is probably eating it right now!

Those who refuse to try anything new might escape poisoning but die of boredom

Find Out More

You can find out lots more about food and its strange and surprising history from these books and websites.

Books

Bartoletti, Susan Campbell. *Black Potatoes: The Story of the Great Irish Famine, 1845–1850.* Boston: Houghton Mifflin, 2001.

Bledsoe, Karen E. *Genetically Engineered Foods.* Detroit: Blackbirch, 2006.

Elliott, Lynne. *Food and Feasts in the Middle Ages.* New York: Crabtree, 2004.

Harbison, Elizabeth M. *Loaves of Fun: A History of Bread with Activities and Recipes from Around the World.* Chicago: Chicago Review Press, 1997.

Ichord, Loretta Frances. *Pasta, Fried Rice, and Matzoh Balls: Immigrant Cooking in America.* Minneapolis: Millbrook, 2006.

Lauber, Patricia. *What You Never Knew about Fingers, Forks & Chopsticks.* New York: Simon & Schuster, 1999.

Schlosser, Eric. *Chew On This: The Unhappy Truth about Fast Food.* Boston: Houghton Mifflin, 2006.

Solheim, James. *It's Disgusting—and We Ate It! True Food Facts from Around the World—and Throughout History.* New York: Simon & Schuster, 1998.

Whitman, Sylvia. *What's Cooking: The History of American Food.* Minneapolis: Lerner, 2001.

Woods, Michael and Mary B. Woods. *Ancient Agriculture: From Foraging to Farming.* Minneapolis: Runestone, 2000.

Websites

Food timeline
http://foodtimeline.org
Read up on the history of hundreds of foods, from basics like bread and nuts (think 10,000 B.C.!) to modern marvels like Chex Mix and Spam. Includes extensive links to historical recipes and other food-related sites.

Weird foods
http://www.foodmuseum.com
The Food Museum is an interesting site about food in all its variety, with lots of information on everything from school dinners to frogs' legs, famine, and chewy squid suppers.

Prehistoric cooking
http://www.channel4.com/history/timeteam/snapshot_cooking.html
A web page about Stone Age food, with a link to some prehistoric recipes.

Medieval cooking
http://www.godecookery.com/godeboke/godeboke.htm
A website with links to hundreds of authentic medieval recipes that have been adapted for the modern kitchen.

The history of candy
http://www.candyusa.org
This fun site from the National Confectioners Association highlights the history of chocolate, gummi bears, candy canes, taffy, and other popular candies, plus trivia, recipes, crafts, and quizzes.

Food pyramid
http://www.mypyramid.gov
This site from the U.S. Department of Agriculture gives daily nutritional requirements based on your age and sex. Click on the "For Kids" section to play a game that tests your knowledge of the food pyramid.

Glossary

ban a law that makes something illegal

banquet a very large, grand feast

bushmeat any forest animal other than game that is hunted for food

cannibals animals that eat their own kind, especially humans that eat other humans

caviar eggs of the sturgeon, a fish that is close to extinction

cholesterol a natural body chemical that makes fat clog up the arteries, causing heart disease

coprolites fossils of excrement, or feces

delicacy something pleasing to eat that is rare or expensive

detoxify to flush toxins, or poisons, from the body

diabetes a physical condition in which there is too much sugar in the blood. Being overweight and eating a poor diet can trigger one kind of diabetes. The other kind is passed from parents to children in their genes.

diet what someone eats and drinks; also short for weight-reducing diet

digest to break down food in the body so it can be used for growth and energy

famine widespread hunger

fasting deliberately not eating when there is plenty of food available

fugu a kind of fish, eaten in Japan, that has poisonous organs

game any wild animal that is traditionally hunted for food

haggis a traditional dish from Scotland that is made from offal (usually the heart, liver, and lungs of a sheep), chopped and boiled inside a sheep's stomach

indigestion an uncomfortable feeling that comes from eating too much or too quickly

kosher a Hebrew word for food that is fit to eat and follows Jewish diet laws

mechanically separated meat shreds of meat removed from bones by machine. It is often used to make cheap meat products

nutrients the parts of food that are good for our bodies, such as vitamins and minerals

offal parts of a food animal that are not muscle, especially organs such as the liver, heart, and kidneys

paleoscatology the study of animals through the examination of scat, or feces

processed partly or fully prepared for eating. Many processed foods contain added chemicals and low-quality ingredients

protein a substance in food that our bodies need to grow and heal themselves

savory not sweet; often spicy or salty

shellfish sea creatures that have their skeletons on the outside of their bodies, such as oysters, shrimp, and lobsters

spices strong flavorings for food, made from plants

sushi a Japanese meal of specially prepared raw fish

toxins unhealthy substances in the body

vegetarian one who does not eat foods containing animal products

Index

Picture credits

The publisher would like to thank the following for their kind permission to reproduce their photographs:

Position key: c=centre; b=bottom; l=left; r=right; t=top

Cover: Corbis/Punchstock.

1: C. Schmidt/Zeta/Corbis; 4r: Viennareport Agency/Corbis/Sygma; 4bl: Darren Sawyer/Bookwork; 5cr: NHPA/David Middleton; 6br: NHPA/Ernie Janes; 7b: Richard Platt; 7tl: Archivo Iconografico, SA/ Corbis; 8tl: British Museum/Heritage Image Partnership; 9t: Gianni Dagli Orti/Corbis; 10br: Ann Ronan Picture Library/Heritage Image Partnership; 11c: Werner Forman/Corbis; 11tl, 11r: Darren Sawyer/ Bookwork; 12bl: Corbis; 12c: 12br: James L Amos/Corbis; 13tr: Topfoto/Werner Archive; 14cl: Bettman/Corbis; 14–15b: Bookwork; 15tr: Edifice/Corbis; 16–17t: Photocuisine/Corbis; 17cr: Charles & Josette Lenars/Corbis; 18 tl: NHPA/Martin Harvey; 18b: Academy of Natural Sciences of Philadelphia/Corbis; 19tr: Warren Photographic; 20cl: Poodles Rock/Corbis;

20tr: Darren Sawyer/ Bookwork; 21c: Rougemont Maurice/Corbis/ Sygma; 21tr: Darren Sawyer/ Bookwork; 21bl: Darren Sawyer/ Bookwork; 22c: Darren Sawyer/ Bookwork; 22bl: Mary Evans Picture Library; 23t, 23cr: Joe Mcdonald/ Corbis; 24tr: Darren Sawyer/ Bookwork; 24cl: James Warwick; 25tr: Reuters/Corbis; 25c: Darren Sawyer/Bookwork; 25b: Michael Freeman; 26bl: Lucky Pierrot/ Handout/Reuters/Corbis; 26tr: Darren Sawyer/Bookwork; 27tr: DK Ltd/ Corbis; 28l: Gerhard Steiner/Corbis; 28tl: Spencer Jones/ Picture Arts/Corbis; 38tr: Hulton-Deutsch Collection; 38bl: Pablo Corral V/Corbis; 39: SPL; 40bl: China Photo/Reuters/ Corbis; 40tr: David Pollack/Corbis; 41tr: Envision/ Corbis; 42tr: Douglas Kirkland/Corbis; 42cr: Darren Sawyer/Bookwork; 42br: Eye of Science/ SPL; 43tr: Mary Evans Picture Library; 44bl: Hamid Sardar/Corbis.